SCHOOL HEALTH SUPPORT SERVICES

S

D0422345

A Best of
Creative Training Techniques Newsletter Book

OPTIMIZING TRAINING TRANSFER

101

Techniques for

Improving Training

Retention

and Application

■ ■ ■

By Bob Pike with Dave Zielinski

Lakewood Publications
A Maclean Hunter Company

Quantity Sales

Most Lakewood books are available at special quantity discounts when purchased in bulk by companies, organizations and special-interest groups. Custom imprinting or excerpting can also be done to fit special needs. For details contact Lakewood Books.

■ ■ ■

LAKEWOOD BOOKS
50 South Ninth Street
Minneapolis, MN 55402
(800) 328-4329 or (612) 333-0471
FAX (612) 333-6526

Publisher: Philip G. Jones
Editors: Bob Pike with Dave Zielinski
Production Editor: Julie Tilka
Production: Carol Swanson and Pat Grawert
Cover Designer: Sandra Saima, Creative Services Inc.

Contents of this book copyrighted ©1994 by Bob Pike and Lakewood Publications. All rights reserved. No part of this publication may be reproduced, stored in a retrieval system, or transmitted, in any form or by any means, electronic, mechanical, photocopying, recording or otherwise, without the prior written permission of the publisher. Printed in the United States of America.

10 9 8 7 6 5 4 3 2 1

Lakewood Publications, Inc., is a subsidiary Maclean Hunter Publishing Company. Lakewood publishes *TRAINING Magazine; Training Directors' Forum Newsletter; Creative Training Techniques Newsletter; The Service Edge Newsletter; Total Quality Newsletter; Potentials In Marketing* Magazine; *Presentations Magazine;* and other business periodicals, books, research and conferences.

Bob Pike, Creative Training Techniques International, 7620 W. 78th St., Edina, MN 55439, (612) 829-1960, FAX (612) 829-0260.

ISBN 0-943210-28-3

Contents

Foreword

This book, *Optimizing Training Transfer*, is one in a series drawn from the best content of *Creative Training Techniques Newsletter*. The newsletter was conceived in 1988 by editor and internationally known trainer Bob Pike to be a one-stop resource of practical "how-tos" for trainers. The idea was (and still is) to provide timely tips, techniques, and strategies that help trainers with the special tasks they perform daily.

When the newsletter began, it was largely fueled by Bob's 20 years of experience in the field and by the best ideas shared by the trainers (more than 50,000 in all) who had attended his Creative Training Techniques seminars. As the newsletter grew in popularity, it also began to draw on ideas submitted by its readers. Today, the newsletter continues to search out creative approaches from the more than 200 seminars Bob and the other Creative Training Techniques trainers conduct every year, and from the newsletter readers.

But no matter where the insights come from, the goal of the newsletter remains the same: To provide trainers a cafeteria of ideas they can quickly absorb, and then choose those that best suit their special needs.

This series of books represents the best ideas from *Creative Training Techniques Newsletter's* six years of publication. It is our hope we've created a valuable resource you'll come back to again and again to help address the unique challenges you face in your job every day.

Sincerely,
The Editors

Introduction

Measuring training's impact on an organization remains one of the most daunting challenges for trainers. Indeed, the days of line managers or training executives accepting "smile sheet" hosannas and "student-days taught" as indicators of training dollars well spent are rapidly ending. Managers who encourage their employees to give up increasingly precious job time to be trained and those who control the training purse strings are demanding harder evidence of transfer of training to the workplace.

That's where *Optimizing Training Transfer* comes in. The book draws together a collection of the best ideas in two closely related areas from the first six years of *Creative Training Techniques Newsletter*. The first is transfer of training, or those strategies trainers apply before, during, and after training events to ensure the training "sticks" and travels beyond the classroom door. Too often, when a trainer announces — in time-honored fashion — "Now, let's review," it's a signal for trainees to set their minds on auto pilot. But interest and retention improve when content review exercises are made more interactive, intriguing, and, yes, entertaining. This book gives you a wide choice of games, memory aids, and creative new spins on familiar ideas to help strengthen retention following review of training modules. There are also examples of how trainers keep the training connection alive by staying in touch with trainees — and their supervisors — long after sessions have ended, including ideas for developing effective job aids.

The second area is evaluation, or measuring training

results. In this chapter you'll find numerous ideas from training practitioners for crafting questions and designing evaluation forms (including sample forms) to get more useful feedback, tips for improving survey response rates, and other ideas about how to better measure training transfer and continuously improve your programs.

In many ways, the hardest work of training begins when your participants exit the classroom door. Supporting and advising trainees in the post-training environment, convincing supervisors to get involved in nurturing trainees' new skills back on the job, and continually working to illustrate — and advertise — training's positive impact on your company are demanding tasks. But, in these times of growing scrutiny, those efforts are more critical than ever if you want to ensure the continued respect, viability, and funding for the training function in your company.

Bob Pike

Section One:
Content Review Tips

David Plantier says illustrations are an effective review tool in classes where trainees must learn multistep sequences, and there's a simple, cost-effective way to get those illustrations: Have attendees create them. Here's how the exercise works:

Plantier, president of Boiler & Combustion Seminars, Bloomington, MN, breaks the class into an even number of groups and asks each group to draw the steps of the process on separate pieces of construction paper. If there are more steps than group members, some trainees must do more than one drawing. He gives the groups four minutes to complete their drawings. Only pictures are allowed, no words.

Plantier then pairs each group with an "opponent," and has the groups stand and face each other in a line. One group shows its drawings out of order while the other group shuffles those holding pictures until the steps are in the correct sequence. If a group didn't have time to complete all of the steps, the opposite group must still put the steps in order and then identify the missing step(s). Plantier then has the groups switch "opponents" and repeat the exercise.

1

Illustrations aid in retention of multistep sequences

2

Let trainees act as instructors to break review monotony

An endless string of slides detailing work processes can be boring and taxing for trainees to sit through. To break the monotony, Lisa Murphy, a trainer of with Hoechst Celanese, Textile Fibers Group, Rock Hill, SC, lets trainees act as the "instructors" during reviews.

In her technical training classes, she uses flow charts supplemented with slides to illustrate steps of a process. After going through the flow chart and completing a question-answer period, Murphy resets the slides back to the beginning and asks a student to be the instructor. Murphy takes that attendee's name tag and seat.

The student then proceeds to reteach the task and explain each slide. Murphy becomes the most inquisitive student in the class. Any question concerning material that has already been discussed is "fair game" for her to ask about. She says it adds humor to the class when she exclaims with a confused look on her face, "I don't understand." Her request for a better explanation encourages the student "teachers" to draw on the board, write definitions on a flip chart, and even call on their classmates for help.

Tapping participants' creative juices can encourage them to use newly learned material while also having fun, says Jack Redfield, a customer contact specialist with Rochester Gas & Electric in Rochester, NY.

Redfield splits his class into small groups and gives each group several sheets of flip-chart paper and markers. He asks each group to pick a benefit they've learned from any other class module and create a magazine or newspaper ad promoting its benefits with text and drawings.

Redfield says the activity is a very effective review tool and that he is amazed at the variety of ideas displayed in the "ads."

3

Creating 'ads' from new material boosts retention

Don't get burned by not knowing your materials is the rather literal point of Verda Christian's admittedly risky technique for reviewing materials that involve memorizing steps, points, or lists.

Christian, sales management coordinator with BB&T, Wilson, NC, gives each participant a wooden match — which varies in length depending on the complexity of the list — and a matchbook to strike it on. For a five-step list she cuts the matches to 1 inch in length. For a list of 25 points she uses full-length fireplace matches.

The class is given three minutes to study materials. Then, on Christian's cue, everyone is told to strike their matches and begin reciting the list aloud. The goal is for each person to finish before the flame burns his or her fingers. Upon completing the list, (or upon losing one's nerve as the flame draws near) participants may blow out their matches.

Prizes may be awarded to everyone who completes the list and has more than a predetermined amount of unburned match remaining.

One way to ensure participants get a chance to share what they've learned is by "passing the hat," says Rick Bennett, a team leader trainer at CSARC in Windsor, CA.

After a topic is covered, or at the end of a session, he asks each participant to write down one valuable concept gleaned from the course, and how it can be used. The ideas are tossed into a hat, box, or other convenient receptacle. After all have contributed, the hat is passed again, and each student removes one note, putting it back and drawing again if it's the one he or she contributed. The ideas may be read aloud. The result: Everyone leaves with at least one useful concept and a way to use it.

5

Passing the hat allows for sharing of best class ideas

6

A 'sharp' way to use dart boards to review

Steve Carcelli, a regional training manager with the drugstore division of Fay's Inc., Liverpool, NY, says a fun way to review without actually saying "now, let's review" is to play darts.

First, he says, simply create a dart board with different subject categories you've covered (see sample on next page) and attach it to a regulation board. Six to eight categories seem to work best. Then divide the categories into point areas — the bull's-eye should include the toughest questions, of course, or even trick questions to get your trainees really thinking. Using point totals of 50 (bull's-eye), 20, 15, and 10, he plays games up to 150 points, giving up to six players per team a chance to throw.

Here's how the game itself works: Create two teams of four to six players each. Player one from the starting team throws a dart. If he or she hits a category, a question is asked of the group based on the points in the category. (A 10-point question is easier than a 20-point question.) If a player misses the target entirely, he or she can shoot until a category is hit.

Teams are given 20 to 30 seconds to answer a question, and the captain provides the answer for the team. If they give a wrong answer, the other team is given a chance to answer and take the points. Once a category question has been answered for a point total, the area is closed — meaning if a player hits the area, he or she loses their turn. Carcelli says this makes the game more challenging as it progresses. Winning teams win a token prize.

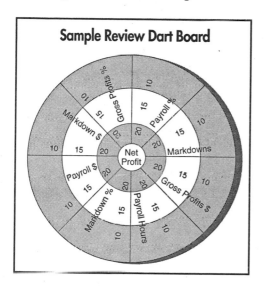

Sample Review Dart Board

7

Pairing students makes for a fun self-review

An hour or so into a session, Robert Schwarz, a professional trainer with the International Association of Lions Clubs, Oak Brook, IL, divides learners into pairs for a self-review process. One member of each duo is instructed to pretend that the other has just arrived and needs help in catching up with what was missed. The first person takes five minutes to update the "latecomer" on everything covered thus far and how it can be applied to his or her work. When the person providing the review is through, the listener steps out of character and states any important information that was missed.

Says Schwarz: "Requiring each participant to articulate what he or she has learned not only enhances memory but greatly reduces my burden to periodically review and consolidate, which is now done more meaningfully by each individual." The exercise, if done occasionally throughout the day, makes an end-of-day review unnecessary, he says.

To help new bank tellers recall a multitude of technical procedures, products, and services, Robin Schaeffer has them develop a learning resource that serves additional duty as a review tool and job aid.

Schaeffer, a staff development specialist at Liberty Bank, Middletown, CT, provides trainees with a pad of paper on which they can take notes during class. As their nightly assignments, she gives participants several 4 x 6 inch index cards and has them condense their notes onto the cards. She also gives each trainee a 5 x 7 inch, two-ring binder in which to put their cards. She quizzes participants the morning following a session on the previous day's material, allowing them to use their index cards during the review.

Schaeffer says the binders are small enough that when a teller is on the job and needs to answer a customer question, she or he can quickly flip to the proper divider and find the card with the information. The binder can be easily updated by removing old information cards and replacing them with new cards explaining the procedure or service.

8

Index-card binder is useful job aid

9

'Yarn link' closure promotes post-class networking

Gary Flanagan, a training director with Continental Insurance in Cranbury, NJ, uses this exercise to provide closure, to validate the performance of trainees, and to promote post-class networking.

When closing a class, Flanagan takes a large ball of yarn and wraps one end around his wrist. He chooses a trainee to compliment on a contribution he or she made to class, be it a sense of humor, pertinent questions asked, or something learned. The ball of yarn is then wrapped loosely around that trainee's wrist, while still attached to Flanagan. That trainee then seeks out another to acknowledge, and so the process goes until all trainees become part of the yarn "web."

Flanagan says the yarn serves as a metaphor for the new connectedness of trainees. "It's a message that even though we remain individuals, the training experience in a sense has made us one. And it's a way of parting with good feelings." The web is also designed to promote post-class networking. "We want trainees to feel even as they leave they'll still be as close as the nearest telephone."

During week-long training courses for new district sales managers, Judy Betheil, a creative writer at Avon Products Inc., Newark, DE, asks participants to write down as many action ideas as they can think of at the end of each learning segment. At the end of each day, have them circle with a yellow highlighter the three ideas they would like to try first back on the job. Each training day has a new action ideas page.

At the end of the week, participants review the ideas they have circled (15 total), and circle in red the three they would like to try first, then circle in green the next three. The activity helps participants prioritize as well as focus only on a few ideas at a time, while leaving new ideas to try for many months to come.

10

Color-coding helps prioritize action ideas

11

Grouping, rating content helps trainees review progress

To gauge how well participants are following material in multi-day courses and make adjustments to her content, Mary Jo Elenburg, a consultant for CommuniSkills in Oklahoma City, asks attendees to print the words "AHA," "HELP," and "BULL" across the top of a sheet of paper at the end of each day. She encourages them to list any concepts that fall into the categories, using these guidelines:

• AHAs are learning points attendees plan to use back on the job. "These are ideas that are new to participants," says Elenburg.

• HELPs are concepts attendees feel need more explanation. "Any time a person thinks, 'I'm confused about...,' it falls into this category."

• BULLs are ideas attendees feel simply were not worthwhile. "A concept that was beaten to death by discussion or explanation, for example, or anything they thought was a bunch of bull," says Elenburg.

After allowing time at the end of each day to complete them, Elenburg collects the unsigned sheets. The following day, she addresses the categories by summarizing the various AHAs, answering the HELPs, and thanking the class for the BULLs and making a note to adjust them for future classes.

As a way to review course material and close his training programs on an entertaining note, Guy Smith, program development and quality assurance representative at Walt Disney World, Lake Buena Vista, FL, holds an award ceremony to celebrate and discuss the most memorable course ideas. Smith gives each participant four ballots for nominating a winner in each of these categories: Idea Most Likely to Be Used, Best Comment Made in Class, Best Volunteer, and Best Activity. Smith then holds a brief discussion about the winners.

12

Celebrating best class ideas a potent review tool

13

'Planned accident' creates interactive review

Victoria Fehrmann, a training and resource consultant for the Missouri Department of Health, Jefferson City, MO, begins her review of course materials by dropping them on the floor.

After she's used a number of overheads, she "accidentally" drops and scatters them. She picks them up and asks a participant to put them back in order — the overheads often follow a sequence of steps in a work process. When the "reorganizer" is finished, Fehrmann projects the visuals and asks the class to help determine if the order is correct. In the process, everyone gets a review of the materials.

This simple exercise suggested by Stuart Summers, division training manager for S.C. Johnson Wax, Ontario, CA, provides a fun review of product information, features and benefits, and major selling points:

1. List a product on the back of a 3 x 5 inch card. Complete one card for each participant.
2. Tape a card to each participant's back.
3. Tell participants to find out which product is on their back by circulating the room and asking the other participants questions. Questions should be phrased so they can be answered with a yes or no response. Some examples could be, "Is the product a new item for our company?" "Does this product cost more than $15?"
4. Allow the group to interact for five minues or less, encouraging them to gather as much information as possible about the products listed on their backs.
5. Have participants guess what product they are "carrying."
6. Reward or praise those who guess correctly.

14

Guessing game well-suited for product review

15

Creative storytelling an effective memory aid

Encourage creative thinking with this review exercise used by Frederick Faiks, a research engineer at Steelcase Inc. in Grand Rapids, MI. Prior to class, he writes two words on the inside of participants' tented name cards. At the appropriate time he has participants turn their tags inside out to reveal the words. He then begins narrating a story related to the course theme, and passes the story off to the first participant, who must continue it while weaving in one of her two random words before passing the story off to the next participant. (Example: "It is 1999 and I just walked into my office. It is not at all like it was in 1994. One primary difference is..." and a participant would use one of her words in a phrase to complete the sentence.)

The story goes around the room twice until all the random words are used. "The brain will try to connect any dissimilar concepts if it is instructed to do so, and some interesting solutions evolve," Faiks says. "It's also a lot of fun and reinforces learning."

To test comprehension midway through a module of instruction, Barbara Quitoriano, a writer and trainer for California School Employees Association, San Jose, CA, passes out a set of questions to half of the individuals or small groups, and gives corresponding answers to the other half. Participants then have to locate the questions that match their answers. This reinforces learning, she says, and also energizes the class.

16

Have groups match questions to answers

17

Give-and-take exercise an engaging roundup

Get one/Give one is an engaging and effective end-of-the-day review, says Bonnie Plummer, executive director of Capital Sierra Administrative Training Center, Sacramento, CA. She asks participants to independently list important ideas or actions they pick up during the training day, then take those sheets across the room to an unfamiliar classmate and compare notes. Participants add one item to their lists from their partner's brainstorm pages, and continue to change partners every two to three minutes. Plummer sometimes uses music, dance steps, and hand motions as people move throughout the room.

Having each participant create his or her own personal review on a cassette tape — instead of just writing key learning points — helps pull participants into the review session and aids retention, according to Terry Paulson, president of Paulson & Associates, Agoura Hills, CA.

Throughout class, participants make lists of key thoughts or quotes that help remind them of meaningful course content. They then record the items on a cassette, five to 10 items at a time. After each set of items attendees add a short musical interlude of their favorite music. The musical interludes allow for reflection on the preceding "keepers." The process is repeated until all material is covered. The result is a personal review tape that won't get tossed aside as written notes sometimes do.

18

Personal review tapes make great job aids

19

Word association inspires high retention

Challenging participants to come up with phrases that rely on word association is a staple in review sessions conducted by John Addy, a trainer with Management Development Specialists, Halifax, England. "Word association reviews tend to have a fairly high retention rate," he says, "because people are coming up with phrases they are going to remember. It also serves as a confidence-builder for attendees, most of whom are pretty surprised by their creative potential."

Addy divides the class into small groups and asks each to prepare a list of 10 random nouns (combination words are also allowed, such as "oven mitts" or "floppy disk"). The groups then swap their word lists and Addy allows them 20 minutes to make an association between each word on the list and a key learning point from the class.

Often, Addy says, it takes a couple of examples from him to get the groups going. He offers the following as a good idea starter:

In a class on effective public speaking, the group might make an association between the skills they have learned and the word "sugar" by writing, "Sugar is sweet. Keep your audience sweet by preparing adequately, maintaining eye contact with everyone, and keeping to your stated time," or "Sugar is an additive sweetener. Visual aids can add something to a presentation, but overindulgence can be a recipe for indigestion," or "Sugar cubes are given to horses as a reward and an incentive. Reward attendees by saying something useful, interesting or thought-provoking, thus giving them an incentive to come again."

When the groups are finished, each must fully describe the associated principle to the entire class.

20

Have attendees write their own review questions

Student-generated reviews are often effective because they encourage attendees to go back over course material they deemed most important. So in classes that meet for a number of consecutive days, Valerie Chapin, metro region trainer, Co-Operations Insurance Co., Willowdale, Ontario, asks students to write their own review questions.

Chapin divides the class into groups of four. At the end of each day she asks each group to generate six questions about the day's materials. The questions are asked of other teams the next morning, with groups competing for points for correct answers.

The exercise fosters independent learning, Chapin says, because participants review the day's materials in hopes of winning the daily contest. It also builds team spirit, and gets the morning off to an energetic start, she says.

If there is material Chapin would like to review but the group didn't cover, she adds those questions to the contest for bonus points.

C rossword puzzles designed around course material facilitate individual and group review in courses lcd by Lee Polk, chief quality engineer for Navistar International of Melrose Park, IL. During a break, he puts a custom-ized crossword puzzle on each student's desk. After the break, each student is given a number. They may exchange numbers if they choose. Polk then asks each student to stand and answer the crossword puzzle question that matches his or her number.

Students with correct answers win a chip that can be exchanged for a prize. Students who give wrong answers must name another student to answer the question. Polk says this review technique has increased retention and cut review time by a third.

21

Crossword puzzle activity cuts review time

22

Quiz features one correct and three 'extremely close' answers

A quiz with one correct answer and three "extremely close" answers for each question serves as an effective review for Mark Hinkel of the Congregational Bible Church, Marietta, PA.

Hinkel breaks the class into groups and passes out one quiz per group. On each quiz a single question is marked for that group to answer. Each group chooses the answer it believes correct, and discusses its choice with the class, with Hinkel serving as facilitator.

Participation is usually excellent, Hinkel says, because groups need to carefully discuss all of the answers before choosing which is the correct one.

Participants learn to take careful notes in classes led by Charles Brougher, director of training for Bryan Foods, West Point, MS.

In week-long training sessions, Brougher starts each morning by asking one participant at random to summarize his or her notes from the previous day. Brougher says it helps get the group back in a training mindset and allows him to reemphasize specific points the note-taker may not thoroughly report.

23

Calling on trainees to share notes keeps them on their toes

24

Log of class ideas acts as review

Asking several people to jot down stimulating ideas from class during each break results in a comprehensive list of ideas for review, says Acey Lampe, communication and training manager with Hallmark Cards in Kansas City, MO. Lampe has each group or every fourth person (depending on class size) write down one important idea from the session before each break.

By the end of class, each person has written one idea. Lampe then uses the idea sheets to summarize the material. "Unless an important idea was left out, there's no need to cover any additional material," says Lampe. "And if an important idea wasn't listed, it's a sign to me that I didn't put enough emphasis on it."

Jim McCoy, area manager with Southwestern Bell Telephone, Irving, TX, uses this game to help students review and to check their understanding of course topics:

McCoy divides the class into groups of three to five people. Each team writes five or six questions on the material just covered. Each team asks questions of another team and rates the oppositions' answers on a scale of one (needs improvement) to five (excellent). A third team listens in and rates the quality of the questions in the same way.

Each team must ask and answer the same number of questions, one question at a time. Awarding prizes to the top team adds flavor to the game, McCoy says.

25

Gauge class progress with Q&A game

26

Deliberate 'bad' presentation is instructive review device

During train-the-trainer sessions, Leigh Chaney, organization development administrator for Columbia Gas Transmission Corp., Charleston, WV, combines review and evaluation by role-playing a deliberately bad delivery style. The technique allows participants to critique and evaluate her performance and to learn from Chaney's "mistakes."

Near the end of the course, Chaney announces, "For the next 15 minutes, I'm going to present some material and I'm not going to do the world's best job. Based on what you've learned, let me know what I did wrong and how I could have improved." At the end of the presentation, the group gives its critique, serving as an effective review of material.

Chaney then asks the class to evaluate her "regular" performance in the session. She says the class is usually more willing to provide constructive criticism if it's been given the chance at a "warm up" critique of her earlier, bogus delivery style.

As an effective review to remind trainees they are in class to learn and not to compete, Rhonda Kirkness, instructor for IBM, North York, Ontario, follows a very technical learning module with the announcement that there will be a quiz. After letting the usual pretest anxiety sink in for a moment, Kirkness then says the quiz is to be completed in small groups because when people work collectively to answer questions, they tend to discuss their answers and learn more through each other.

When the class completes the quiz, students volunteer their groups' answers to the various questions. If necessary, Kirkness reveals the correct answer and explains the rationale, allowing groups to correct their quizzes.

27

Ease anxiety with group quiz

oretta Gutting, manager of
Southwestern Bell in St. Louis,
uses a crossword game as a review
exercise. Gutting writes one con-
tent-related word in the center of a
piece of graph flip-chart paper.
Students must build on that word
and subsequent words in a crossword puzzle fashion.

Students can use any letters to
build words. Gutting says it's
proven to be a great way to review
or brainstorm topics.

F											
U								I			
N	O	N	J	U	D	G	M	E	N	T	A	L
								T			
								E			
	B	R	A	I	N	S	T	O	R	M	
	E							A			
	V							C			
	I							T			
	T	E	A	M	W	O	R	K			
	W										

Vito Scotello, management development representative for Target Stores, Minneapolis, propels his students into an imaginary future as a way to review materials and give participants an opportunity to feel good about learning.

Scotello divides the class into small groups at the close of his sessions and asks trainees to imagine they are five years in the future, and that because of the skills they've learned in the workshop they have become incredibly successful — so much so that they are the subject of a television "Newsbreak."

Scotello allows the groups 15 minutes to write the "newsbreak," and encourages wild ideas based on class content. Each group's spokesperson delivers the message. (Using a microphone at the front of the room adds to the excitement.)

Scotello says this exercise can be highly effective with intact work teams because their group goals are already set. They often project great results for the company based on their efforts.

29

Glimpse into future challenges trainees to retain content

'Traveling review' creates instant content experts

Consultant Michele Deck suggests this exercise to help participants review, without announcing that a review is about to take place:

Deck asks four volunteers to go to separate corners of the room and each post an area of content about which they feel they could answer a question. He then breaks the class into small groups and has them travel to each corner of the room and ask a question about the subject posted.

If the person in the corner correctly answers the question, he or she joins the traveling group and someone else from the group stays in the corner as the new "content expert." Deck has the small groups continue to travel from corner to corner, changing places and asking questions.

G racy Luby, director of staff development for Oklahoma City Public Schools, asks participants to create their own memory aids for review purposes. For example, to remember six principles of retention, one participant came up with the mnemonic "FTD PM," or "flowers in the afternoon."

The F stands for "feeling," T for "tension builds retention," D for "degree of original learning," P for "practice," and M for "meaning."

Luby says creating individual memory devices enhances retention because participants are actively involved in creating the device. These personalized review tools can also be shared with the entire training group.

31

Creating their own memory enhances trainees' retention

32

'Who Am I?' parlor game an active review

For an active review, Linda Waterman, a California-based training consultant, uses this variation of the old parlor game, "Who Am I?" She writes various concepts from the course on name tags or Post-it Notes and sticks one on the back of each participant. Participants then move around the room and ask questions of one another to identify the procedures, concepts, or key learning points from the class that they are wearing on their backs.

In a class that meets for one week a month for three months, Dallas Wiley, industrial service engineer for Culligan International, uses this review procedure:

Before each week, he develops a crossword puzzle using process terminology and definitions of materials covered in the course, in addition to locations/names/trivia pertaining to individual students.

Interaction and discussion among participants is necessary to work the puzzle. Wiley says it helps attendees to debrief how they've applied the previous session's material, and allows them to reconnect prior to starting the next week's classes.

33

Crossword puzzles encourage student interaction

34

Balloons put pop into wrap-up sessions

Stella Spalt, manager of management development for the American Red Cross in St. Louis, puts some pop into her review sessions by challenging participants to burst balloons and then answer the review questions written on slips of paper placed inside.

This can be done individually or with teams, with prizes provided for correct answers. A variation is to use balloon color to signify question difficulty and the number of points awarded. For instance, red balloons might be worth five points, blue balloons worth 10 points, and so on.

This "three-minute" exercise used by Lea Toppino and Sonia Diaz, trainers at John Alden Life Insurance Co., Miami, is an effective review tool that keeps trainees from suffering from information overload in classes that require quickly absorbing a lot of information.

After presenting information about company departments and functions in their customer service training classes, Toppino and Diaz split the group into two teams. The instructors post flip charts around the classroom, each labeled with the name of a department or function. Then, each team is given a stack of Post-it Notes with statements pertaining to the different departments/functions they have learned about. Here are a few sample statements: "This department is in charge of employee training," "This department manages the 401k," or "This team handles recruiting new employees."

The goal is for teams to place as many statements as they can on the appropriate flip charts within three minutes. When time is called, the instructors debrief by reading the statements on each flip chart to ensure they're in the right places.

35

'Three-minute' review eases information overload

36

Varied review formats appeal to more learning styles

Sharon Paredero of Pacific Bell uses a variety of review techniques in lieu of the "predictable and boring Q&A." When she varies the review formats, she finds the sessions are more effective, and appeal to a wider variety of learning and thinking styles. Here are two of Paredero's favorites:

■ *Collaboration / Articulation:* Divide the class into groups of two or three. Give each person a topic or subtopic and ask everyone to take a turn telling others in their small groups everything they know about that topic. Continue until all members have a turn. You may want to set time limits for each rotation. At the end, ask participants to post any leftover questions or concerns about the topics for the rest of the class to discuss.

■ *Olympics:* This review technique works well for classes that last five days or more. On the second day of training, divide the class into even-sized teams of three to five people. Tell them you are holding an Olympic event, and that you will keep score for the duration of the class. There are two ways for a team to accumulate points: (1) If the individual you direct a question to answers it correctly without references, that team receives three points. (2) If he or she cannot answer the question, it is opened up to the entire class. The first person who answers it correctly receives one point for their team.

(Noisemakers are useful for trainees to signal if they want to answer a question. A buzzer or bell is a good way to signal when time is up.)

Day three is run the same as day two. For the remaining days of the class, give each team time to formulate a certain number of questions to ask other teams. They may use references to formulate the questions. Each team presents one question at a time to the other teams. Scoring is handled the same as day two.

At the end of the class, total the scores. Present the prize to the winning team. Paredero recommends an edible prize because it is not expensive, and usually the winning team shares the prize with the other teams.

37

'Musical chairs' review energizes trainees

To share the best ideas from a series of sessions or course units, Susanne Moore asks each participant to think of the most powerful ideas drawn from the course, write them on separate sheets of paper, and tape them to the walls throughout the room.

Moore, sales training and management development specialist for Great Western Bank, Chatsworth, CA, then turns on some music and has trainees play a modified version of musical chairs, called "musical review." She lets the music play while participants walk around the room in a clockwise direction to build up some energy. When she turns off the music, she has participants read the nearest idea sheet to the group. Participants remove those ideas from the wall and repeat the exercise until all the ideas have been read — and all but one trainee has lost their "sheet" and sat down.

"By sharing someone else's idea, multiple ideas are reinforced," Moore says. "And adding music and movement creates an energizing review."

In new-employee orientation training, where employees often feel tentative about asking questions, Susan Partee uses a technique to get them immediately involved and focused on class material.

Partee, a training assistant with O'Reilly/Ozark Automotive in Springfield, MO, types questions concerning class content on index cards, one question per card and one card per participant. After class introductions she passes out the cards and explains that each participant is responsible for answering — in writing — the question on his or her assigned card, and assures everyone their question will be covered in class before they are called upon for an answer.

Then, at 15 to 20 minute intervals, she asks who has question 1, etc., (questions pertain to areas just discussed) and the participant with that question reads it aloud, along with the answer.

Partee says the exercise also serves to capture the attention of attendees waiting for an answer to their own most pressing questions.

38

Assigned questions ensure trainee attention

39

Staggered quizzes make good 'bookend' reviews

In order to evaluate and review what attendees have learned from a unit of training — and to provide a forum for participants to share differing points of view — Don Watts twice administers a "true/false" quiz that pertains to course material.

Before the unit begins, Watts, an instructor at Mount Royal College, Calgary, Alberta, administers the quiz — usually about 20 questions long — and then pairs trainees to compare answers. The partners are encouraged to discuss the reasons for their answers and, if they wish, convince their partners to change answers. At the end of the exercise, the partners sign each others' test papers and put the quizzes aside.

At the completion of the learning unit, the participants retake the same quiz, and the partners again meet to exchange answers as before. They are again encouraged to discuss reasons for their answers and to convince their partners to change.

Watts then follows up with a full-group discussion on the test items and other questions the participants may have regarding the completed unit.

40

Summary statements prep trainees for workplace grilling

There are some forms of training that you just know will generate questions from trainees' coworkers when they get back to the job. Total quality management is one of those topics, says Bob Mathews, though there certainly are others. In an effort to make sure participants are ready for those questions, Mathews, a customer service manager for Oscar Mayer Foods Corp., Ontario, spends the last portion of his sessions asking each trainee to generate a short but complete answer to the query, "What is total quality management?"

These "elevator speeches," as Mathews calls them, are presented to the entire class. Trainees are encouraged to alter their individual responses if they feel a peer came up with a better description. Mathews says the exercise arms people with good responses for on-the-job grilling and also helps him to make sure trainees understand key learning points.

41

Dose of competition sparks greater interest

With salespeople as his main training audience, David Blunt, international training and sales development manager for Alcon Surgical Labratories in Fort Worth, TX, believes injecting an element of competition into review sessions not only sparks interest among participants, but also improves retention.

So rather than the standard practice of giving a test at the end of each day of his five-day training sessions, grading it, and then reviewing results the next day in class, Blunt cuts out individual questions from tests and places them in an envelope. The envelope is then passed among small groups, with each small group removing one question and posing it to another group. Each group receives the same number of chances to answer questions. If the question is not answered correctly by the targeted group, all other groups get a chance to answer. At the end of the exercise, the group with the most correct answers receives a small prize.

Blunt occassionally adds a few twists, like introducing a soft or spongy ball for teams to toss to warn a team a question is coming.

Kaye Sanders capitalizes on people's appetite for lottery games in her review sessions. She includes one of her self-designed lottery tickets in each packet of course materials, or simply tapes a ticket to every desk or chair. A corresponding number to each of the tickets is included in Sanders' large "lottery box."

At review time, Sanders, training coordinator with the Jacksonville Electric Authority, Jacksonville, FL, asks each participant to write three or four review questions. She then selects a lottery number from the box and asks the student holding that matching ticket to answer a question relating to the course material. If he or she needs help, Sanders encourages the group to provide assistance.

Once the question is answered correctly, the person initially selected picks a number from the box and poses a question from his or her own list to the ticket holder. The lottery continues until everyone in the group has a chance to ask and answer a review question. Sanders says trainers should also prepare a list of questions in case trainees exhaust their own lists.

42

Lottery tickets an effective review incentive

43

Ensure no one 'leaves' with unresolved questions

Rick Kitchen uses a "review tree" to ensure he addresses all pertinent questions before class ends — particularly questions of trainees reluctant to speak up for fear of asking "silly" questions.

Kitchen, a training supervisor with C.U.C. International in Dayton, OH, first draws a tree with multiple branches on a sheet of flip-chart paper. The session's main topic forms the "trunk" of the tree, and individual categories of the topic make up the branches (see graphic on opposite page). In a recent session, for instance, meeting management skills was the main topic, with the branch categories being planning, idea development, motivation, decision making, and problem solving.

The branches — which remain covered by slips of paper until the category is addressed in class — are drawn without leaves. During breaks or after a session, Kitchen asks those trainees with questions that haven't yet been answered to write the question on a large Post-it Note, then stick the note/leaf on the branch subject it best fits. "We ask them to post it even if the same question has already been posted," Kitchen says, "to help gauge how much more review is needed." It's also an effective way for shy or reluctant trainees to get questions answered.

Questions that don't fit categories are placed on the "ground" — the bottom of the flip-chart page — as fallen leaves, and are also addressed during the review.

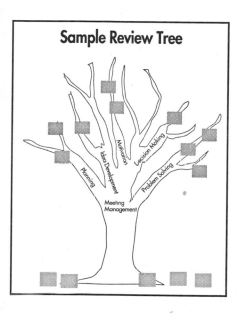

Sample Review Tree

44

Take the temperature of trainees' mastery levels

Quick, snapshot measures of how trainees are mastering material give trainers immediate feedback and allow for "just-in-time" adjustments to improve the learning curve.

At the beginning of a five-day training course, Jim Espich, national training manager with Smith and Nephew United in Largo, FL, gives each trainee a list of learning objectives and a "thermometer" for each objective. Trainees use the thermometers to gauge their own progress in achieving objectives. The four levels, starting with the lowest "degree," are: Overview Level, Introductory Knowledge Level, Working Knowledge Level,

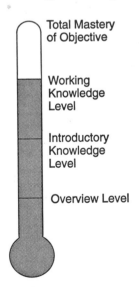

Total Mastery
of Objective

Working
Knowledge
Level

Introductory
Knowledge
Level

Overview Level

and Total Mastery of Objective.

Espich reviews each trainee's thermometer at the end of each day, and the group compares thermometers every two days to see if there are objectives where everyone is still "lukewarm." If a trainee's thermometer shows he is still at the "working knowledge" level on the third day of class, for example, Espich can work with that person, or assign other trainees to help bring him up to speed. The goal is 100 percent mastery of all goals.

Candy incentives give review shot of flavor

Kathy Wright adds flavor to computer course reviews by hiding a piece of candy under each student's keyboard. Wright, a senior education instructor for Unisys in Wellington, New Zealand, uses candies that come in several shapes or colors, such as those shaped like cartoon characters or jelly beans.

She programs students' computers to display a message when they sign on, instructing them to look under their keyboards. The message goes on to explain that the candy will determine which review question each student will answer. People with green pieces may be asked to demonstrate a word-processing command, while those with red candies may be asked to review a data entry procedure.

The method also allows Wright to "stack the deck," so less-confident trainees get less-challenging questions, and more experienced users get tougher ones.

To energize participants and summarize key points at the end of a training session, Mariana Luce, a trainer with Arbitron Co. in Beltsville, MD, uses a fast-moving game she calls "Bump":

• Break people into groups of four to five.

• Give each team a one-minute timer (or a facilitator can keep time with a watch), flip-chart paper, and five markers.

• The object is to list single words that summarize key training points (Example: A point about giving good feedback might be abbreviated with "timely.")

• To win, a team needs to list the most words in one minute.

• Give everyone a marker, so they can write words on their team's sheet as quickly as possible.

• After one minute, all writing stops.

• Teams then "bump" or cross out from their lists any words that appear on any other team's sheet.

• The team with the longest list of unduplicated key words wins.

Says Luce: "Everyone usually leaves the session laughing and energized, even if winning is the only prize."

46

Challenge trainees to sum up points in single words

47

When repetition is necessary, make it interactive

It's been said that ownership of information only takes place after it's been restated at least 21 times, says Carolyn deRobertis, a senior training specialist for Automatic Data Processing, Parsippany, NJ. Students won't always tolerate that sort of repetition from an instructor, however. So deRobertis makes a game of repetition, and gets participants to teach themselves.

She asks students to sit in a circle to review features of a product, service, or procedure. One person is selected to offer a feature. The next person repeats the first feature and adds another. This continues around the circle, with each person repeating all features offered and adding to the list.

One way deRobertis uses the technique is to create a strong company image in employees' minds by offering the company as the "product" being discussed. The first person might say, "We've been in business for X years." The second would repeat that, and could add, "We've had tax-filing products for X years," and so forth.

When Diane Raden overheard a participant wishing out loud that he could receive periodic reminders of course lessons to keep them fresh in his mind, she acted on it. Raden, a member of the sales education department at Valley National Bank, Phoenix, AZ, now composes a brief summary of each critical learning point on a piece of memo paper and includes a pertinent graphic or cartoon and a one-line motivational quote.

For several weeks following training sessions, Raden sends each attendee these "reinforcement" memos. The memos aid retention as well as create a sense that the instructor cares.

48

Memos keep session lessons 'evergreen'

49

Super balls put new bounce into review

As a quick and simple review technique, Ruth Wenzl Gerber, owner of The Training Edge in Lincoln, NE, uses two dozen fluorescent "super balls," the super-charged variety that can easily bounce to the ceiling.

At the end of class, she asks participants to share their biggest "aha" from the training curriculum — the learning point that had the most meaning to them or "from which they'll get the greatest return from the smallest investment." She tosses each participant a super ball as he or she recites a point.

Lori Smith gets all participants in her classes involved in reviews by allowing them to act as experts in her "Ask the Expert" exercise.

At the end of her management practices courses, Smith asks attendees to write a difficult question or scenario related to the course topic and put it in a basket. She then draws the submissions one at a time and opens the floor for comments and input. The collective answer from all contributors becomes the "expert," Smith says. She says this exercise allows participants to share their knowledge and experiences involving real-world situations.

Give attendees the floor for greater participation

A brief review exercise can be a great way to get things moving after lunch or at the beginning of the second day of a session. Willy Ashbrook, national sales manager for Deluxe Sales Development Systems in Lakewood, CO, uses this group technique:

• Break trainees into three groups.

• Ask each group to formulate two questions pertaining to materials covered. They may use textbooks, notes, flip-chart pages on walls, and so on.

• After questions are written, put away reference materials. The review is a "closed-book" exercise.

• Instruct Group A to ask Group B a question.

• Have Group C critique Group B's answer, using a 10-point scale. Ask Group C to explain how Group B's answer could have been improved to earn a top rating of 10.

• Next, allow Group B to pose a question for Group C to answer, then have Group A evaluate the response.

• Repeat the process until every group has asked one question of all other groups.

• Provide rewards for members of the group with the highest total score, as determined by their peers.

To aid retention and appeal to trainees' visual intelligence, Caryn Evans asks them to create a "graphic journal" of the key points from a session. She says the technique is based on the accelerated learning theory.

At the end of each learning module in her two-day seminar, Evans, a project consultant with the Principal Financial Group in Des Moines, IA, asks participants to use colored markers and a notebook with unlined paper to draw graphic symbols of the concepts they found most relevant in that preceding module. She gives them two minutes to draw the graphic.

The graphic representation serves as a summary participants can refer back to as a quick review, Evans says.

52

'Graphic journal' offers quick visual summary

53

Response cards serve as instant survey tools

Milli Morisette, a trainer for the Southern Region Children's Service Division, Eugene, OR, gives each student a set of three 5 x 8 inch cards labeled, "yes," "no," and "undecided," at the beginning of class. Throughout the session she makes statements — some of them course-related, others playful or trivial — and asks participants to respond by holding up the appropriate card. Statements vary from contextual to ones like, "Of all the places I could be right now, this classroom is where I would choose to be."

The technique helps students review their knowledge of materials while getting to know one another, Morisette says. Attendees sometimes request the chance to ask the class a few questions of their own.

Gary Thompson uses this twist on review ideas. At the end of a session, he asks individuals or groups to formulate questions based on material covered, then place those questions in a shoe box. Thompson, a customer service representative for ADP Automotive Claims in Etobicoke, Ontario, places a number of small prizes — pens, chocolates, magazines, and so on — equal to the number of questions in another box.

The prize box is passed around the room until a participant decides to draw a prize. The participant shows the prize to the rest of the class, and announces that a right answer to the next question drawn will win it. The question box is then circulated, and the individual or group wishing to contend for that prize draws a question. If two groups or individuals want the same prize, they both draw questions, and the first with a right answer wins. The review continues until all questions/prizes are exhausted.

Competing for small prizes adds spice to review

55

Make follow-up letters more than 'thank yous'

The typical session follow-up letter is just a "thank you" and a summary of the key points covered in class. But it can be much more, says Bob Tomayko. "Make the follow-up letter an effective review tool that challenges trainees to practice what was taught."

Tomayko, senior corporate trainer for Blue Cross & Blue Shield of Georgia in Columbus, GA, accomplishes this feat by taking a creative approach to the process and adding competitive incentives. Some of the tactics he uses include:

• After a session on effective listening skills, he sends attendees a taped message covering key points on becoming better listeners. He includes a riddle at the end of the message, and tells them if they correctly solve it and return an answer they will get a small prize.

• In a follow-up letter to a writing program, Tomayko violates all the writing principles he discussed in class. He challenges people to edit, rewrite, and return the letter. Tomayko rewards them with a special pen.

• As a follow-up for a creative thinking class, he includes a cryptic crossword puzzle that lists all the main subjects. Attendees who complete the puzzle get a prize.

Kathleen Burke-Scheffler uses this review game in multiple-day training sessions. At the end of the first day of class, she has each student write two or three questions from the day's content. Questions can be in multiple choice, true/false or fill-in-the-blank form. Burke-Scheffler, a trainer with US West in Minneapolis, collects the questions and adds a few herself.

At the start of day two, she uses the questions for a takeoff on "Hollywood Squares." She simulates the tick-tack-toe game show by setting up three chairs, asking three volunteers to sit on the floor in front of them, three to sit in the chairs, and three to stand behind them.

Each of the nine "celebrities" is given a card with an "X" printed on one side and an "O" on the other to tape to their bodies as questions are successfully answered.

She asks for two volunteers to serve as contestants and has them pick members of the "celebrity" squares to answer the questions in turns. Contestants respond with "agree" or "disagree" to the panel's response as they try to form a tick-tack-toe. Remaining trainees are given agree/disagree cards to flash to aid in contestants' decision-making.

56

Hollywood
Squares
takeoff
recaps
long
sessions

57

'Tick-tack-toe Bingo' tests trainees' memories

Almost anything is more fun to learn if you make a game of it. Joyce Davis combines two familiar games — tick-tack-toe and Bingo — to test the memories of her trainees.

Davis, a training coordinator at Nintendo of America in Redmond, WA, prepares a list of terms and their definitions, culled from the course material. At the end of the session, she gives each trainee a list of terms numbered one through nine and a sheet with a tick-tack-toe grid printed on it. She then has attendees write a number from one to nine randomly in each square of the grid.

Next, Davis recites or uses an overhead to randomly show one definition at a time. Trainees must

Sample Tick-Tack-Toe Bingo

match the definition to the numbered term on their lists, so the corresponding number can be crossed off the tick-tack-toe grid. When three numbers in a straight or diagonal line are crossed off, the trainee can call out "Bingo!" (see graphic on opposite page). In order to win a prize, the trainee must also correctly recite the definition to each of the three winning terms. An incorrect match of definition and term means the game continues.

Section Two:
Evaluation Techniques

R ather than using standard paper evaluations, Deb Donnelly has a more interactive and energizing way of assessing the pre- and post-training knowledge level of participants. In her class covering principles of the quality certification process ISO 9000, she places the numbers one through 10 (each written boldly on a sheet of colored construction paper) on the floor around the room's perimeter, and asks participants to stand near the number that represents their current knowledge of the topic.

Donnelly, a quality facilitator with Eastman Kodak Co. in Rochester, NY, records those numbers. She repeats the exercise at the course conclusion to get a reading on how much participants feel they've learned, "and to give participants feedback and reinforcement for their learning efforts," Donnelly says.

58

'Stand up' evaluation offers glimpse of knowledge levels

59

Ask trainees to judge program context as well as content

Participants can provide valuable feedback on the context of a training course as much as they can on its content, says Bill Wright. That's why, as part of an overall evaluation guide, he asks attendees to take note of such items as noise levels and possible distractions, as well as the start and stop time of the event (see form below).

Sample Evaluator's Guide

Session Title: _____

Date: _____

Trainer's Name: _____

Start Time: _____ Stop Time: _____

Evaluator's Name: _____

Number of Trainees: _____

Training Location: _____

Noise Level (circle one):

      Low   Medium   High

Space (circle if NOT adequate):

- Enough room for books
- Chairs comfortable
- Lighting sufficient
- Other:_____

Temperature (circle one):

      Cold   Hot   Acceptable

Distractions (circle those that apply):

- Windows
- Busy area
- Other: _____

Other comments about the training location and/or setup: _____

Wright, a training and development specialist for Western Surety Co., Sioux Falls, SD, asks participants to complete the form as the training session begins, but to not include additional standards on the form, or to give the trainer a "pass/ fail" type of grade for training skills not noted on the form. That type of evaluation is done later on a different form.

60

Informal evaluation forms can elicit better response

Informal evaluation forms can sometimes garner a better response rate and better feedback than more traditional forms.

For example, Coleen Kelsall, a staff development consultant for the Department of Housing in Australia, hangs several sheets of butcher paper on the walls of her classroom with questions such as, "What did you like most about the program?" or "What one thing would you say needs improvement?" written at the top of the paper. She invites attendees to write responses either right on the paper or on Post-it Notes that can be stuck to the appropriate sheet.

The butcher paper, Kelsall says, often results in a better response rate to the evaluation questions and is more fun for participants. The technique also seems to encourage attendees to be more expansive in their answers, she says.

The next time you design an evaluation form, consider asking participants to evaluate more than just the trainer and the session content. Include questions that also ask attendees to evaluate their own participation performance. Questions like, "How well did you get involved?" or "How well did you work at applying content to your own job situation?" may prompt insightful responses.

Also ask each participant to evaluate the rest of the audience. Questions like, "Did they get involved?" "Did they work?" or "Did they learn?" can elicit powerful and useful feedback.

You can also help shape the behavior of participants if you hand out evaluation forms early in the session so participants know in advance what you'll be asking them to critique at the session's close.

61

Have trainees rate their own class participation

62

To-the-point rating system draws high response

A short evaluation form that uses visuals in addition to a standard rating system garners more responses and proves to be much more fun to complete, according to trainer Peggy Putnam.

At the conclusion of courses, Putnam distributes the form (illustrated below). She says that compared to longer forms she has used in the past, the form enjoys a much higher response rate because it's short and to the point. "And besides a chuckle, we do receive valuable feedback on which to base an evaluation of the presentation."

Presentation Evaluation Form

Great · Good · O.K. · Fair · Poor

One thing I learned that I can apply is:

_____

This presentation could be improved by:

_____

Other comments:

_____

Kay Albrecht modifies the usual course evaluation process to give participants some perspective on how others view the class and as a review.

Albrecht, a senior partner at Innovations in Early Childhood Education, Houston, TX, asks each person to fill out an evaluation form. She then has teams get together, compare responses, and formulate a group evaluation. Participants often sympathize with views different from their own after hearing explanations.

Next, each group presents its evaluation to the class. Again feelings will differ, reinforcing the point that people can reach different conclusions and learn different lessons from the same experience.

The method also deflates some of the criticism aimed at content, process, or facilities, Albrecht says, because an opposite view is often reported. And, because participants discuss class material, it acts as a review.

63

Method shows students hear same lesson, but different message

64

Mini-evaluations keep content on track

Feedback from mini-evaluations at the end of each segment of a longer session helps Kathy Pillion make changes to better meet the needs of the group as the course progresses rather than after the course — when it's too late for that group.

At the beginning of class, Pillion, manager of planning and development at Coles Myer in Gepps Cross, South Australia, gives each attendee a pad of Post-it Notes and a handout of rating scales (see below). At the end of each segment, Pillion asks participants to use three Post-its to evaluate: (1) the value of the session, (2) session clarity, and (3)

Evaluating Each Activity

For the activity just completed, decide on...

Value	Clarity
3 = Vital	3 = Crystal Clear
2 = Good to Have	2 = Reasonable
1 = A Waste of Time	1 = Unclear

Comments

Write it on a Post-it Note and stick it on the flip-chart paper on the wall. Thank you for your honest feedback.

any other comments. She has participants post the notes on a piece of flip-chart paper hung in an easily accessible place in the room, and leaves them up so participants can read each others' ratings and comments.

Pillion says the information tells her instantly if the group has grasped the essence of the segment, whether more or fewer group activities are needed, if energizers are needed, or even whether the room's temperature needs to be changed.

65

Trainee 'reunions' can improve training's application

The true test of any training program is how well it translates into on-the-job effectiveness. In a plan that extends the training for participants and also gives trainers useful feedback, Mike Canfield, training manager for Pinellas County in Clearwater, FL, reconvenes participants one week after his 28-hour training and again three weeks later.

The idea is to have participants demonstrate how they used ideas from the training back on the job, and provide suggestions to others in the group who may be having difficulty translating training tips and knowledge to their own job situations. Canfield says if some trainees have difficulty in finding time for such an informational reunion, sessions can be held after hours or even on weekends for those interested in attending.

An exercise called "Super Stars" enables participants to give each other immediate positive feedback in a presentation skills workshop led by Kathleen Davis and Wylecia Wiggs at the American Heart Association National Center, Dallas, TX.

Participants give five-minute presentations to the group. Each person in the group completes a "super star" form for each presenter (see below). Participants write the name of the presenter in the center of a small yellow note pad shaped like a star. Then they write five good things about the presentation, one in each of the star's points. Observers are given a minute following each presentation to complete the star and pass it to the presenter. Presenters receive suggestions later in private from the facilitators.

Instant peer feedback focuses on positives

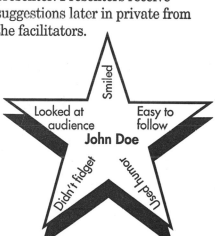

67

'Mapping' content ensures linear path to conclusion

Once Bob Bonnell thinks he has a design for a training presentation near completion, he gives it a final test called "strategy mapping." Using a variety of symbols, Bonnell, a senior vice president of marketing for Strongput Inc. in Baltimore, maps the course of the presentation on paper from start to finish, being careful to account for any hazards, conflicts, or other unexpected turns he might encounter (see graphic). "The goal," he says, "is to ensure that I am navigating to a clear objective in my courses."

Mapping helps clarify his direction and allows him to identify the critical path including theme, teaching tools, potential "rocky roads," "dead ends," and what he calls "rivers of refreshment."

Strategy Mapping

Gerald Zwaga sends a questionnaire to students four months after each class, asking whether the training was useful and appropriate. Zwaga, a technical consultant for Aetna Insurance, Hartford, CT, also writes to attendees' supervisors informing them that the employee was asked to fill out the evaluation.

This correspondence reinforces the importance associated with training and also helps to encourages communication between trainees and their supervisors regarding training, Zwaga says.

68

Evaluation strengthens bonds between trainees, supervisors

69

Daily reviews serve dual purpose

To encourage students to get answers to their questions during multiday sessions, Colleen Kelly Laich uses daily evaluation sheets. The forms cover all of the day's topics, asking the usual questions about whether materials were useful and well-delivered.

What makes the forms uniquely useful, says Laich, a supervisor of commercial underwriting and regional evaluations for Nationwide Insurance, Columbus, OH, is the additional space after each topic for students to ask anonymous questions. Besides encouraging students to ask questions that might otherwise go unanswered, the sheets also serve as point-by-point refreshers, reminding students of points they may have meant to ask but overlooked.

To assist participants in thinking of questions and comments, sheets have "catalyst phrases" printed on them: "That's new to me," "I didn't know that," "I disagree," and so forth.

The daily evaluations also allow trainers to adjust materials, pace, and delivery style to better fit the tastes and needs of a particular group, she says.

During extended training sessions, Thad Standley asks attendees to keep "evaluation journals." Journals allow trainees to reflect on what they've learned and on how a course can be improved as they progress through the it, rather than straining to remember everything at the end of the course. At the end of a session, Standley, evaluation chairperson for the Nebraska Association of Student Councils, Lincoln, NE, collects the journals, reviews them, then mails them back to trainees.

The journals also act as a review tool back on the job.

70

Evaluation 'journals' track trainees' comments

Evaluation of Neal Whitman's
train-the-trainer courses are
decidedly unique. Whitman borrows
the signature trait of movie critics
Gene Siskel and Roger Ebert —
that of "thumbs up" and "thumbs
down" — in evaluations. And,
though it may seem a bit Pollyanish
to think that a training program
should be the "most exciting,
personally rewarding experience" in
the lives of your trainees, it's
exactly the model Whitman, a
trainer at the University of Utah's
School of Medicine, Salt Lake City,
asks his trainees to hold his sessions up against. "It gives trainers-
to-be something to shoot for when
they train," he says.

At the end of his sessions, Whitman asks participants to think of an
experience in their lives that
matches the description above, then
compare his program to that
experience. He gives attendees a
postcard with a line drawn between
a thumbs-up and thumbs-down
icon, and tells them to mark the line
where the program falls.

After collecting the cards, Whitman distributes another set of
postcards, these with his name and
return address. He asks attendees
to reconsider the comparison in a
month and return the cards, after

they've had time to implement the new skills they've learned. Though names are not required on the cards, Whitman asks attendees to record the last four digits of their social security numbers for a before-and-after comparison.

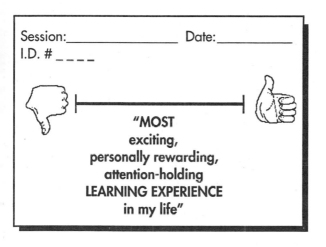

Session:_____ Date:_____
I.D. # _ _ _ _

"MOST
exciting,
personally rewarding,
attention-holding
LEARNING EXPERIENCE
in my life"

72

Listing skills of best, worst instructors yields valuable data

As a way to evaluate her own skills, trainer Victoria Baugh asks her classes — usually those being trained as trainers — to individually list the traits of the worst and the best instructor they've ever had. The lists are tallied and posted on two flip-chart sheets at the front of the class, stimulating discussion about ways that trainers can avoid negative behaviors.

Baugh, a trainer in the Naval Technical Training Center at Treasure Island in San Francisco, CA, then compares these traits to those listed in the instructor evaluation instrument used in class to determine whether that instrument needs any adjustment.

A sk participants to write their titles (in addition to their names) on evaluation sheets for feedback that shows learning needs in certain groups, says Donna Smith, a training specialist for Dun & Bradstreet Software, Atlanta, GA. The technique is especially useful in classes attended by people from a variety of backgrounds within the company, she says, and can be used to modify material so everyone is getting what they need.

For example, Smith says, in a general course on sales skills, evaluations may reveal that account executives say they need more cold-calling skills while product representatives feel too much course time was spent covering those skills. The result: Break the class into groups and teach each group what they want to know.

73

Including job titles makes evaluation forms more usuable

74

Follow-up question forms determine impact of training

Follow-up questionnaires are an inexpensive way to determine the impact of training, redundancy in training, and transference of training to the workplace, says Helena Whyte.

She believes questionnaires — mailed three months after delivery of training — can garner much more valuable feedback than can a phone call or even a personal visit, and are easier to complete on a widespread basis. Whyte, training coordinator for the industrial hygiene group at Los Alamos National Laboratory, Los Alamos, NM, says her experiences with questionnaires have taught her these lessons:

• The follow-up questionnaire serves as a mechanism to remind trainees and supervisors of the objectives of the training and the final performance of the training.

• The questionnaire must be designed so that trainees and supervisors only need a few minutes to answer if improvement has been noticed on the job, which skills are being practiced, and which skills are getting rusty.

• The follow-up also provides trainers with an opportunity to ask for a work sample. The information provided is helpful in revising course content and reinforcement exercises.

- The Microsoft Excel software application program can be used to personalize letters to trainees. The follow-up letters and questionnaires can be prepared with end-of-course certificates and mailed on a specific later date, usually three months after course completion.

- A higher rate of return often results when questionnaires are returned to the instructor rather than to the training manager. Whyte says anonymity *has not* increased the number of returned questionnaires. Even when identification is optional, most trainees prefer to identify themselves.

- Supervisors typically provide anecdotal data of training impact in conjunction with the questionnaire. Additionally, Whyte's experience shows that trainee and supervisor perspectives of training impact don't differ much.

75

Ask trainees to write post-course memos to supervisors

Do you wonder what trainees are really getting from your programs? Susan Partee finds out by asking them to write post-course memos to their managers.

Within a week of a course's conclusion, Partee, a training assistant at O'Reilly Automotive, Springfield, MO, sends participants a letter requesting specific feedback to her and to attendees' supervisors. She includes guidelines to simplify the task. The instructions ask participants to address their memos to the supervisors who approved their course attendance, and to present course highlights (three or four main topics). They are asked to be candid about whether the material was interesting and useful, and to conclude with a personal note about how the information applies to their particular positions.

Partee also encourages students to include a brief "thank you" to tell their supervisors the learning opportunity was appreciated. She also requests that a copy of the memo be sent to her, to ensure she gives trainees proper credit for attending.

The "Crumple and Toss" test is a safe midpoint evaluation of a training session's progress, says Ellie Rilla, county director of the University of California Cooperative Extension Office, Novato, CA. She hands out paper and asks participants to write how they think the session is going, any changes they think are needed, and what they still hope to learn.

When participants are finished writing, they crumple their papers and toss them to someone else. The tossing continues for several seconds, until the evaluations are thoroughly mixed. Participants then take turns opening and reading aloud the papers they are holding. Rilla lists what is said on a flip chart.

The flying paper wakes up participants and gives them a chance to vent their frustrations, she says. And the anonymous assessments give the trainer an idea of class progress, and how best to use the remaining course time.

Tossing class evaluations around elicits candid responses

77

Group-completed evaluations provide quality feedback

When trainees collaborate in small groups to fill out course evaluation forms, the feedback is of far better quality than when completed individually, says Olaf Nippierd, director of customer service at Dun & Bradstreet, Melbourne, Australia.

At the start of each course, Nippierd divides participants into groups. Each chooses a leader. At the end of the class, each leader is responsible for turning in a group evaluation. In addition to standard evaluation questions about the presentation and the value of the course content, it also asks for a team objective and a three-point action plan. Where applicable, the team is asked to describe what it would like included in future training sessions.

Copies of the evaluation are distributed to team members and related management personnel. The tactic is particularly useful when assessing the effectiveness of new courses and in developing inexperienced trainers, Nippierd says.

Smile sheets — those end-of-session evaluation forms that elicit "how'd you feel about the course" responses — don't always provide trainers with actionable information. Here's how two trainers go about getting higher-quality evaluations:

■ Rick Wise, training specialist at Dauphin Deposit Corp., Harrisburg, PA, has each participant address an envelope and place an evaluation form inside, which he mails to them a week after the course ends. Although he gets less than 100 percent response, the delayed feedback is usually far more helpful than smile sheets for evaluating his skills and the program's effectiveness, he says.

■ Rick Migliore, labor relations and training coordinator for the Pennsylvania Office of the Attorney General, goes beyond smile sheets with a personal phone call follow-up. He calls each participant to ask what elements of training they're using on the job. It's important, though, to inform training participants up front that they will be called, *when* they might be called, and specifically what they will be asked, Migliore says.

Delayed-response evaluations capture more useful feedback

79

Well-targeted evaluation forms yield best data

A ndy Sheldon, manager of training for Royal Bank of Canada, Toronto, passes on a story that illustrates the need for clear objectives to garner accurate feedback from attendees.

"A man once rode into a western town. As he passed through, he noticed targets painted on the sides of all the buildings, each with a bullet hole directly in the bull's-eye.

Amazed by the marksmanship, the visitor walked into the local saloon to inquire about the targets. 'Oh, that's Crazy Joe,' the bartender replied. "He lives east of town. Just follow the gunshots."

Sure enough, as the visitor went east he saw more targets with bullet holes in the bull's-eyes. As the visitor came into a clearing, he finally sighted a man with a rifle over his shoulder. Suddenly the man aimed and fired the gun at a large tree in the center of the clearing. Then he calmly put down the gun, grabbed a can of paint and a brush, and proceeded to paint a target around the bullet hole."

Sheldon says to get honest evaluations to help improve your training, you need to communicate that objective to attendees before they fill out evaluations and also state that objective on evaluation forms.

Getting attendees to fill out full-page course evaluations can be difficult. So Jenny Huffer encourages 100 percent participation by using a simple grid with columns for rating coverage of each course topic (see graphic below).

Huffer provides colored dot stickers to participants, who can place the dots in any of the five rating areas or on the lines in-between. The process takes just a few minutes and avoids the tedium of an essay-style evaluation, she says. The forms serve as partici-pants' "ticket out of class." It's so quick it can be done daily during a multiday session, she says, or even multiple times during the same day or at break times during a shorter session.

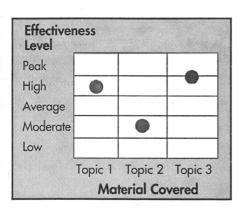

80

Simple evaluation grid increases response rate

81

It pays to evaluate knowledge before and after courses

Sal Haqqi, senior instructor for IBM Canada Ltd., uses a pre- and post-attendee evaluation for course content to determine whether he's met his training objectives.

At the beginning of a class, Haqqi introduces participants to the course objectives, discusses them briefly, then asks students to evaluate their current knowledge of the topic. At the close of the class, he asks students to rate themselves again. Haqqi says the evaluation helps him determine whether his students learned the course objectives, and if he actually delivered information he promised.

Sheena Foley, training and development coordinator for Thrifty's, follows up her training sessions by mailing participants a summary of the course evaluations. She also sends out a "recap memo" of the key learning points of the program in addition to a 90-day to six-month follow-up evaluation form to get feedback from participants about skills they're using on the job.

She finds that by having the two contacts — session evaluations and the summary of learning points — more application of training content occurs.

82

Follow-up contacts reinforce application of content

83

Self-evaluation hones trainees' critiquing skills

At the end of a three-day training refresher on coaching and critiquing skills at Canada's Boehringer Ingelheim Ltd., participants are asked to rate themselves on a scale of 0 to 100, based on their contributions and involvement during the course.

After scores are recorded, each participant stands and explains why they rated themselves as they did. The group then provides constructive input — their opinions as to whether the person had been too generous or too tough on themselves. Trainers Vicki Dickson and Janice Ryan say the exercise helps reinforce the techniques used in coaching, and helps to remind the "coaches" what it's like to be on the receiving end of feedback.

Live audience feedback, solicited immediately at the end of class, can garner more valuable content than written evaluations, says Elaine Tanabe, human resource development manager at AT&T.

Tanabe asks participants to complete a written evaluation as well, but because she makes a special effort throughout her classes to develop a rapport with participants, she feels they're just as apt to give honest, oral feedback to help enhance future courses. Although first attempts at this face-to-face feedback takes some bravery, Tanabe says she often gathers information that would never have shown up on the written evaluation form.

84

'Live' feedback often more valuable than written forms

85

Props allow trainees to signal learning progress

Vern Jorgensen, an instructor for Southwestern College, uses color-coded blocks — one-half painted red, the other half painted green — to gauge at a glance where students are in terms of comprehension or task completion during a presentation in his courses.

Jorgensen gives each participant in the class a block and asks them to indicate whether they're comfortable with a new concept, or have completed an assigned task, by using these signals: the green side of the block turned up means, "I'm ready to move on." The red side up means, "Hold on. I need just a little more time."

Participants often wonder if their evaluation of a training course is actually ever used to improve a class. Showing participants that evaluation forms are carefully reviewed and that their input is needed, wanted, and acted upon encourages them to take evaluations more seriously, says Robert Mitchell Jr., human resources specialist with Chemical Waste Management. He suggests starting a training program by presenting the evaluation form and indicating changes that have been made in the course because of past feedback.

86

Show trainees evaluation feedback is taken seriously

87

Collecting 'critical incidents' has dual value

A technique that can be used for both evaluation and analysis is to collect critical incidents or individual real-world stories. In analysis, ask people to describe an incident that shows a deficiency, then use that incident to show how a problem can be resolved through training.

The same critical incident strategy can be used after a program on a 30-, 60-, or 90-day follow-up. Call participants and ask them to "tell a story" about how they've taken a learning point from the seminar and applied it to their jobs.

Repeat this exercise a few times, and you'll have accomplished two things: One, you'll have a good reading on the course in terms of its transfer to the job. Two, you'll collect an assortment of anecdotes that can be used in your current training to show its application to the real world.

W hat could be handier than a hand? Debra Turner of Corning Inc. says hands make a good, quick, five-point evaluation scale. She gives participants two or three items she wants evaluated, such as usefulness of content or pace of presentation. She has participants put their hands behind their backs and, at the count of three, show their finger rating — one being low, five being high.

This can be done quickly to rank several items and give the instructor an instant read on the seminar's impact, making midstream changes possible.

88

Show of hands provides instant assessment

89

Ask trainees and managers to preview program purchases

When training officer Leonie Robertson tests an off-the-shelf training program on a trial basis, she sets up a "working party" consisting of participants and their bosses. Each pair selects a part of the session and provides feedback as to its applicability and relevance.

Robertson encourages new ideas and criticism, and the pairs formulate a half-page report serving several purposes:

1. It stimulates discussion.

2. Participants become self-motivated, since they'll likely be recipients of the program.

3. It ensures that technical topics not only contain essential information, but that they are presented at the level of participants.

4. It encourages self-development.

5. Attendees form questions on content they can follow up on later.

Jean Borill, a development manager for Westpac Financial Services, determines how effective her training has been against set parameters, such as increased productivity. Borill recommends following these five guidelines to make training more accountable:

1. Involve managers in determining the productivity measurement prior to the training course.

2. Ask managers to clearly communicate their expectations of results to participants.

3. Set a realistic timeframe for measuring.

4. Ensure that participants develop a personal action plan, including the "what," the "how," and the "when" of implementation.

5. Reward all those who produce the required results — but let managers present the rewards.

Clear guidelines can ensure training's effectiveness

91

Small gifts improve evaluation response rates

Whenever Nancy Pyle, a registered nurse/educational instructor at Marion General Hospital, conducts a training program, she offers each participant a reward for completing the course evaluation form.

The rewards are typically small promotional items she's received free from sales representatives who call on the hospital, such as pen lights used in checking patient charts at night.

According to author Michael LeBouf, the greatest management principle in the world is "what gets rewarded gets done." Irene Brooks, a computer specialist for USDA National Finance Center, uses the principle to encourage participants to complete evaluations and turn them in on time. As evaluations are turned in, she provides gift coupons issued on strips of paper good for a free beverage or snack from the cafeteria.

In large classes, she sets up the reward coupons in a drawing, with many blank slips of paper and some gift coupons together in a basket that participants draw from as they turn in their forms.

It probably can't be stressed enough that communication with the supervisors of your participants improves your course material and facilitates transfer of classroom work back to the job. Here are two strategies for improving that communication link:

■ Michael Randazzo, a distribution instructor for Public Service Electric and Gas Co., schedules periodic visits to managers of participants to hear complaints, answer questions, and to uncover possible training needs. Whenever possible, he makes the visits two weeks prior to a training program or within one week following a program to help ensure manager satisfaction with the training or to uncover any last-minute needs.

■ Leonard Orzechowski, a training supervisor also with Public Service Electric and Gas Co., creates an on-the-floor follow-up for every training program he conducts. The scheduled meeting with the participants and their supervisors enhances the link between classroom content and application on the job.

92

Follow-up visits with trainees, supervisors enhances application

93

Segmented evaluation form provides fresh feedback

When a course is long and the material complex, handing out evaluation forms at the end usually begets only vague, summary-type compliments and complaints. Particularly when conducting a course for the first time, you want a great deal of feedback so you can adjust the course, says Michael Smith, director of training and development for Metcalf & Eddy. So he developed a form that participants use throughout courses he gives (see graphic on opposite page).

Participants rate eight segments of the course immediately after experiencing each section. The content segments are each rated on four aspects on a 1 to 5 scale:

- Utility Scale (ranges from "Left Me Cold" to "Very Useful")
- Interest Scale (ranges from "Dull" to "Very Interesting")
- Change Scale (ranges from "Change or Delete It" to "Don't Change")
- Presentation Scale (ranges from "Should Improve" to "Well Done")

"We run the risk of negative comments when some things have not yet fallen into place, but that kind of information is better than never hearing about problems at all," Smith says.

The illustration shows the four evaluation scales Smith uses and the matrix on which participants rate each key content point of the course against those four criteria. (The matrix usually includes eight key points from the course.) Smith has participants rate each key section at its completion, filling in the numbers in the appropriate columns.

Segmented Evaluation Form

	Left me cold		OK		Very Useful
Utility Scale					
	1	2	3	4	5

	Dull		OK		Very Interesting
Interest Scale					
	1	2	3	4	5

	Change or Delete		OK		Don't Change
Change Scale					
	1	2	3	4	5

	Should Improve		OK		Well Done
Presentation Scale					
	1	2	3	4	5

Content	Utility	Interest	Change	Presentation
Key Point 1				
Key Point 2				

94

**Separate
critique
of trainer,
content
on forms**

Evaluation forms should clearly differentiate questions regarding the quality of the material and the quality of the seminar leader, recommends Clair Leboeuf, a senior consultant for Peat, Marwick, Stevenson, and Kellogg in Canada.

Her forms have separate sections that enable her to quickly see whether both aspects — the material and the trainer — meet the high performance standards of her organization.

Instead of having a "one size fits all" evaluation form, Elizabeth Schiff, senior training manager for the American Academy of Ophthalmology, customizes workshop evaluations for each course. For example, when teaching a five-part course on needs analysis, she divides the form into five specific sections, one for each part of the course.

The technique allows her to include content-specific information that tells her which pieces of the workshop are the most and least useful for participants.

95

Customize evaluation forms for more precise data

Requiring signed forms is unpopular, but pays dividends

It's frustrating to receive course evaluation forms with comments worthy of follow-up, but with no names on the forms. Charles Hansen, training specialist with John Hancock Mutual Life Insurance Co., tells participants they won't get a certificate of course completion unless he receives a signed evaluation form from them.

"Sometimes I'll want to get more information about the background of a comment, or ask how I can improve upon a low score, or explain the reason why the class was structured a certain way, but have no way of doing it without a name," he says.

Some people may not be initially happy about the policy, Hansen says, so it's a good idea to take a few minutes to explain the rationale behind the decision to require signatures.

"I convince them that I am not vindictive and they should feel free to give me low marks or make negative comments. In fact, I tell them that saying the course was perfect doesn't help me at all because I always try to make some improvement each time I teach a course. The candid and honest comments I receive from students help me to do that."

R ichard Urisko, senior manager of personnel at Hitachi America Limited, has an effective way of developing critical incidents to use in training and in a newsletter he distributes to participants. He follows up one month after each training program with a letter asking each participant to "tell a story" about how the training proved effective. Urisko publishes the stories he receives in the newsletter. The strategy reinforces the training for participants, and develops ongoing interest in the course from people yet to take it. Additionally, people are rewarded for applying course content back on the job by seeing their names and stories in print.

97

Follow-up newsletter keeps training interest alive

Cynthia Howe Merman, a St. Louis-based consultant, says in addition to evaluating program material, trainers must constantly evaluate their own performances. One way to do that, she says, is to identify your maturity level and strive to keep improving through experience and education. Here are the four stages of maturity Merman says all trainers experience:

1. *The Toddler Trainer* is, at the start, excited, unsure, and scared. He or she stays close to secure objects such as lecterns, training manuals, handouts, and visual aids.

2. *The Teenage Trainer* is ready for action and is annoyed by limits set by others. This trainer relishes the training scene, likes being center stage, overloads the design, and easily runs over time with enthusiasm. He or she assumes everyone else is equally enthusiastic and energetic.

3. *The Twenties Trainer* recognizes his or her responsibilities, prepares well, and establishes a realistic program and pace. This trainer is calm and competent.

4. *The Timeless Trainer* is challenged by synergism. This trainer works with trainees and supervisors to integrate the program into everyday work life.

Evaluation doesn't have to be a grim activity. Susan Raycroft, a California-based trainer, lightens things up during evaluation by awarding participants amusing certificates before the "formal" evaluation takes place.

She creates certificates for categories like best shopper, most obnoxious role-play, etc., and participants themselves help create categories. It helps remind people not to take themselves too seriously.

99

Amusing certificates add levity to evaluations

100

Encourage attendees to exclude personal feelings from feedback

When it comes to evaluation, Vicki Ford, regional training manager for the Crystal Co., believes in divorce. She encourages participants to divorce themselves from feelings about her personality and to focus strictly on the course content when filling out evaluations. Why does she do this? People tend to praise a program simply because they are taken by a trainer's personality. Emphasizing the course content in evaluations, not the trainer's personality, frees people to be more critical and make valuable comments that can help trainers make necessary improvements in course material.

Getting narrative feedback from participants is often more telling and precise than a numerical, 1-10 rating system. Kathy Hutchings, a trainer with the Oklahoma City Clinic, writes the words *soaring, sailing, swimming,* and *sinking* on a flip chart at evaluation time and then passes out note cards.

She asks participants to identify sections of the program they feel soared, the sections that sailed, and the sections that seemed to swim or sink, and why. Hutchings says the narrative evaluation exercise can be used as either a day-by-day evaluation for long programs, a section-by-section evaluation for shorter ones, or as an overall rating for an entire course.

101

Narrative feedback often more telling than numerical ratings

About the Author...

Robert Pike has been developing and implementing training programs for business, industry, government, and other professions since 1969. As president of Creative Training Techniques International Inc., Resources for Organizations Inc., and The Resources Group Inc., he leads over 150 sessions each year on topics such as leadership, attitudes, motivation, communication, decision-making, problem-solving, personal and organizational effectiveness, conflict management, team-building, and managerial productivity.

More than 50,000 trainers have attended Pike's Creative Training Techniques workshops. As a consultant, he has worked with such organizations as American Express, Upjohn, Hallmark Cards Inc., IBM, PSE&G, Bally's Casino Resort, and Shell Oil. A member of the American Society for Training and Development (ASTD) since 1972, he has served on three of the organization's national design groups, and held office as director of special interest groups and as a member of the national board.

An outstanding speaker, Pike has been a presenter at regional and national conferences for ASTD and other organizations. He currently serves as co-chairman of the Professional Emphasis Groups for the National Speakers' Association. He was recently granted the professional designation of Certified Speaking Professional (CSP) by the NSA, an endorsement earned by only 170 of the organization's 3,800 members.

Pike is editor of Lakewood Publications' *Creative Training Techniques* newsletter, author of *The Creative Training Techniques Handbook*, and has contributed articles to *TRAINING Magazine, The Personnel Administrator*, and *Self-Development Journal*. He has been listed, since 1980, in *Who's Who in the Midwest* and is listed in *Who's Who in Finance and Industry*.

Want More Copies?

This and most other Lakewood books are available at special quantity discounts when purchased in bulk. For details write Lakewood Books, 50 South Ninth Street, Minneapolis, MN 55402. Call (800) 328-4329 or (612) 333-0471. Or fax (612) 333-6526.

More on Training

Powerful Audiovisual Techniques: 101 Ideas to Increase the Impact and Effectiveness of Your Training $14.95

Dynamic Openers & Energizers: 101 Tips and Tactics for Enlivening Your Training Classroom $14.95

Optimizing Training Transfer: 101 Techniques for Improving Training Retention and Application $14.95

Managing the Front-End of Training: 101 Ways to Analyze Training Needs — And Get Results! $14.95

Motivating Your Trainees: 101 Proven Ways to Get Them to Really Want to Learn $14.95

Creative Training Techniques Handbook: Tips, Tactics, and How-To's for Delivering Effective Training, 2nd Edition $49.95

Creative Training Techniques Newsletter: Tips, Tactics, and How-To's for Delivering Effective Training $148/12 issues